MESSI
SECOND EDITION

Abbeville Press Publishers

New York · London

A portion of this book's proceeds are donated to the **Hugo Bustamante AYSO Playership Fund**, a national scholarship program to help ensure that no child misses the chance to play AYSO Soccer. Donations to the fund cover the cost of registration and a uniform for a child in need.

Text by Illugi Jökulsson

For the original edition
Design and layout: Árni Torfason and Ólafur Gunnar Gudlaugsson

For the English-language edition
Editor: Joan Strasbaugh
Production manager: Louise Kurtz
Design: Ada Rodriguez
Copy editor: Amy K. Hughes

PHOTOGRAPHY CREDITS

AFP: p. 9 (Messi's family)

Getty Images: front cover (David Ramos), p. 2 (Jamie McDonald), p. 8 (Simon Bruty), p. 9 (Jamie McDonald), p. 11 (Sabella: Claudio Villa), p. 17 (Di Stéfano: Keystone), p. 18 (Kempes: Getty Images), p. 19 (Maradona: Bongarts), p. 21 (Denis Doyle), p. 22 (Rexach: Allsport UK), p. 28 (Luis Bagu), p. 28 (Xavi, Iniesta, Messi: Jasper Juinen), p. 30 (David Ramos), p. 32 (Bagu Blanco), p. 34 (David Cannon), p. 34 (Mark Thompson), p. 36 (Bob Thomas), p. 39 (Shaun Botterill/FIFA), p. 42 (David Ramos), p. 43 (Christof Koepsel), p. 44 (Müller: Allsport UK), p. 44 (Messi: David Ramos), p. 46 (Bagu Blanco), p. 50 (David Ramos), p. 51 (David Ramos), p. 54 (Maradona: David Cannon), p. 55 (Bale: Denis Doyle), p. 55 (Zlatan: Harry Engels), p. 56 (Europa Press), p. 58 (Romero: Mike Stobe), p. 58 (Zabaleta: Matthew Lewis), p. 58 (Mascherano: Jamie McDonald), p. 58 (Rodriquez: Jamie McDonald), p. 58 (Di María: Elsa), p. 59 (Buda Mendes), p. 59 (Stanley Chou).

Shutterstock: back cover, p. 9, p. 10 (Rijkaard: mooinblack), p. 10 (Guardiola: Maxisport), p. 11 (Messi: Maxisport), p. 12 (Jiri Sebesta), p. 13 (Messi: catwalker), p. 14 (Richie: Helga Esteb), p. 15 (Riquelme: David Alayo), pp. 16–21, p. 25 (Maxisport), p. 26 (Natursport), p. 28 (celebration: Luis Bagu), p. 33 (Maxisport), pp. 40–41, p. 48 (Denis Vrublevski), p. 52 (Above: Natursport), p. 52 (below: Maxisport), p. 53 (Zlatan: Maxisport), p. 53 (Maradona: cinemafestival), p. 54 (Messi: mooinblack), p. 54 (Ronaldo: Natursports), p. 54 (Neymar: almonfoto), p. 55 (Suárez: mooinblack), p. 61.

Wikimedia Commons: p. 17 (Stábile: photographer unknown).

Please note: This book has not been authorized by Messi or persons associated with him.

First published in the United States of America in 2015 by Abbeville Press, 137 Varick Street, New York, NY 10013

First published in Iceland in 2014 by Sögur útgáfa, Fákafen 9, 108 Reykjavík, Iceland

Second edition
10 9 8 7 6 5 4 3 2 1

A previous edition of this book was cataloged as follows:
Library of Congress Cataloging-in-Publication Data
Illugi Jökulsson.
 [Lionel Messi. English]
 Messi / by Illugi Jökulsson.—First edition.
  pages cm.— (World soccer legends)
 Translated from Icelandic.
 Summary: "Profiles the Argentinean soccer star of FC Barcelona, Lionel Messi. Discusses his early childhood success, his training with the Barcelona junior team, and features fun facts like his favorite foods and his pet peeves"— Provided by publisher.
 Includes bibliographical references and index.
 1. Messi, Lionel, 1987—Juvenile literature. 2. Soccer players—Argentina—Biography—Juvenile literature. I. Illugi Jökulsson. Lionel Messi. Translation of: II. Title.
 GV942.7.M398I45 2014
 796.334092—dc23
 [B]
                          2013045843

For bulk and premium sales and for text adoption procedures, write to Customer Service Manager, Abbeville Press, 137 Varick Street, New York, NY 10013, or call 1-800-ARTBOOK.

Visit Abbeville Press online at www.abbeville.com.

CONTENTS

MESSI AND ARGENTINA

The editors of Katla Books in Iceland sought out soccer specialists from around the world and asked them to choose the ten greatest players of all time. They were asked to base their choices on the athletes' personal skills and their influence within the world of soccer. The results are as follows:

	Player	Nation	Year
1	**Messi**	Argentina	2005–
2	Pelé	Brazil	1957–1971
3	**Maradona**	Argentina	1977–1994
4	Cruyff	Netherlands	1966–1977
5	Puskás	Hungary/Spain	1945–1962
6	**Di Stéfano**	Argentina/Colombia/Spain	1947–1962
7	Garrincha	Brazil	1955–1966
8	C. Ronaldo	Portugal	2003–
9	Platini	France	1976–1987
10	Zidane	France	1994–2006

The dates indicate the years the player participated in national games.

Diego Maradona

Although the order in which these legends are listed can be debated, most people would probably agree that Lionel Messi, Diego Maradona, and Alfredo Di Stéfano all belong in the top ten.

And this tells us two things. First, the fact that three of ten players on the list were born in Argentina shows that soccer truly runs in the blood of Argentines. Argentina is probably even more soccer-crazed than soccer superpowers such as Italy, England, Brazil, France, Germany, or the Netherlands. Secondly, Lionel Messi's position on this list shows that he is generally recognized as a major soccer genius and one of the best to have ever played the game.

And Argentina entrusts Messi with the task of delivering them a third World Cup victory, sooner rather than later!

Lionel Messi of Argentina during the international friendly match between Sweden and Argentina on February 6, 2013, at the Friends Arena in Stockholm, Sweden.

SIMPLY THE BEST!

Frank Rijkaard, Barcelona coach 2003–2008

"It's amazing what Messi can do with the ball. And he's still young and that's great news because that means he can only get better as a soccer player. Soccer should make people happy and that's what Messi does, he makes people happy, he makes people enjoy the game."

Pep Guardiola, Barcelona coach 2008–2012

"Messi is the best. I think I've been very fortunate to have been his coach. He is a unique soccer player. The throne is his. Only he decides when he steps down."

Alejandro Sabella, Argentina coach 2011–2014

"What Messi does . . . well, we will probably have to find new adjectives in the dictionary to describe him."

WHERE IS HE FROM?

Lionel Messi was born on June 24, 1987, in Rosario, the third largest city in Argentina.

Argentina

The country is in South America and is very big—the eighth largest country in the world. In fact, it covers an area as large as the following 12 European countries combined: Iceland, Norway, Sweden, Denmark, Germany, the Netherlands, Belgium, France, Britain, Ireland, Spain, and Portugal. Yet the population is "just" 41.5 million. That's slightly smaller than the population of Spain and somewhat larger than the population of Poland. The population of Argentina is the third largest in South America, after Brazil and Colombia. Argentina's capital city is called Buenos Aires.

A Turbulent History

The first native inhabitants settled the south of South America several thousands of years ago. Around AD 1500 the Spaniards started colonizing the continent, and believing that there were great sources of silver to be found in the area they named it *Argentina*—which translates into "Land of Silver." They turned out to be wrong, there was in fact little silver in Argentina, but the name stuck.

In 1816 the people broke with Spain and founded a republic. People emigrated from

VENEZUELA

COLOMBIA

BRAZIL

BOLIVIA

CHILE

PARAGUAY

Rio de Janeiro

Rosario

Buenos Aires

URUGUAY

Montevideo

ARGENTINA

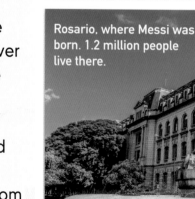

Rosario, where Messi was born. 1.2 million people live there.

many European countries to Argentina, but Spanish remained the main language.

Argentina has seen some troubled times: the country's history is marred by violent disputes and unrest. The country was, for instance, ruled by the *Junta*, a tyrannical military government, from 1976 to 1983. At that time a certain young couple was settling down and starting a family in the city of Rosario.

The Messi Family

This young couple was Jorge Messi and Celia Cuccittini. He worked in a steel factory, and she held various jobs in addition to taking care of the home. In 1980 they had a son called Rodrigo. Another boy was born in 1982 and was given the name Matías. Jorge and Celia were ordinary, diligent working-class people with very little money to spare.

Their third son was born in 1987. He was a normal boy who had a very normal childhood. His father and brothers were great soccer enthusiasts, as most Argentines are, but the little one didn't seem very keen. He preferred to play with glass marbles and collect picture cards.

Messi's parents, Jorge and Celia, with his fiancée, Antonella.

A Fateful Day

When the boy was four years old his father and brothers were out in the street playing soccer in front of their house. Surprisingly, the little one waddled out and wanted to join in, and of course he was welcome to. His father and brothers were in for a bigger surprise.

"We were shocked to see how good he was," Jorge said later. "And he'd never played before."

This was the first time, but definitely not the last, that the boy charmed people with his ball skills. Because this little boy was Lionel Messi.

THE LITTLE LION, CRAB, AND RABBIT

Hello!

In 1984 the popular singer Lionel Richie released the single "Hello" and it topped the charts worldwide. This was a slow and romantic song that appealed especially to people in love.

Jorge and Celia Messi probably slow-danced a few times to this song when they went out dancing. Three years after the song was released they had their third son and, as the story goes, they decided to name him after the singer.

The name Lionel means "little lion" and fits Lionel Messi perfectly!

Lionel Richie

Sensitive and Caring

Lionel Messi was born on June 24, which means that his zodiac sign is Cancer. People born between June 22 and July 22 all belong to the sign of Cancer.

Some believe that zodiac signs determine a lot about a person's character and personality.

used to play together on the Argentine national team.

Riquelme is an attacking midfielder with fantastic skills and he was in fact playing for Barcelona when Messi first arrived there. Riquelme was then transferred to Villarreal in Spain, and later to Boca Juniors in Argentina. He has nothing but praise for his young compatriot. "He's simply a genius," Riquelme says of Messi. "The most amazing thing is that he runs faster with the ball than without it. I don't know anyone else that can do that."

That's probably only superstition, but people born under the sign of Cancer are said to be sensitive, very caring, and intuitive. And even though they do enjoy the company of others, they are also very independent.

Messi's Chinese zodiac sign is the rabbit. Rabbits are said to be good friends, generous, friendly, artistic, humble, stubborn, and slightly moody.

Shared Birthday

The most famous soccer player who shares Messi's birthday happens to be an Argentine as well. His name is Juan Ramán Riquelme and he was born June 24, 1978. The two of them

Juan Ramán Riquelme

SILVER IN THE FIRST ATTEMPT

Soccer in Argentina has a long history. The Argentines played their first national game in 1901, against Uruguay, and won, 3–2. It was the first public national game in the world outside the United Kingdom, where the modern soccer game originated. No other two countries have competed in national games more often than Argentina and Uruguay, who have met more than 200 times. The Argentines also constantly compete with their other neighbor Brazil, and their games are always filled with passion and fighting spirit. In 1921, the Argentine team became South American champions for the first time. They have won that competition, which is now called the Copa América, a total of 14 times, most recently in 1993.

Soccer's first World Cup was held in Uruguay in 1930. The Argentines played terrifically and when they entered the finals, facing their rival Uruguay, they achieved a 2–1 lead in the game's first half. In the second half, however, the home team rallied and defeated Argentina, 4–2. The Argentine team took home the silver.

Argentine forward Alfredo Di Stéfano was one of the greatest soccer players in history. Here he scores with Real Madrid against Harry Gregg, the Manchester United goalkeeper, at Old Trafford. Unfortunately, Di Stéfano never played for Argentina in the World Cup.

Stábile was Argentina's first World Cup star and an admirable and daring goalscorer. However, the only national games Stábile played in were during the 1930 World Cup. He had an incredible goals-per-game ratio, scoring eight goals in four games. After the 1930 World Cup, Stábile played for European teams for many years. He coached the Argentine national team from 1939 to 1960.

GUILLERMO STÁBILE
1905–1966
National games, 1930: 4
Goals: 8

He is cool, he is Stábile.

ALFREDO DI STÉFANO
B. 1926
National games, 1947: 6
Goals: 6

MEAGER YEARS

Argentina did not participate in the final rounds of the three World Cups that took place between 1938 and 1954. The team, however, was nearly undefeated in South American competition during the same period. Moreover, one of the greatest goalscorers of all time, Alfredo Di Stéfano, came of age during those years. He was an extremely agile and clever utility offensive player and is considered one of the greatest players in history. Unfortunately, Argentina's national team was able to enjoy his skills for only a little while. Di Stéfano played a mere six national games for Argentina. After that he left the country and played for Colombia and Spain. He is most famous for his amazing winning streak with Spain's Real Madrid club.

TWO GOLD MEDALS

The people of Argentina went crazy for soccer in the 20th century, and the passion associated with the game in Argentina is almost unparalleled. People say that for Brazilians soccer represents the joy of life, but for the Argentines the sport takes on the importance of life itself—it symbolizes life's struggles. It was therefore painful for the Argentines, who had not managed to win a World Cup, to see their neighbors in Brazil become champions in three of the four World Cups played between 1958 and 1970. But things changed in 1978, when Argentina hosted the competition.

A TIGHT-KNIT GROUP

The 1978 team from Argentina did not have any international stars in its ranks. It was, however, tight-knit and bursting with fighting spirit. The swift Daniel Passarella led a powerful defense, and Mario Kempes scored the highest number of goals of any player. Kempes made two goals following the stoppage time in Argentina's spirited victory over the stellar team from the Netherlands.

GOLD MEDAL AT 1978 WORLD CUP

Final, June 25
Buenos Aires, Argentina

ARGENTINA – NETHERLANDS
3–1

Kempes 38', 105'   Nanninga 82'
Bertoni 115'

Ubaldo Fillol, goalkeeper
Olguin – Luis Galván – Passarella – Tarantini
Ardiles (Larrosa, +66') – Gallego – Kempes
Bertoni – Luque – Ortiz (Houseman +75')

Coach César Luis Menotti

MARIO KEMPES
B. 1954
National games, 1973–1982: 43
Goals: 20

Mario Kempes was Argentina's brightest star at the 1978 World Cup. Kempes played for many teams over a long career and finally retired in 1999.

MARADONA!

The Argentine team was no longer lacking a massive star eight years later—by that time Diego Maradona had entered the scene. Maradona is generally acknowledged as one of the greatest talents in the history of soccer. He was a tremendously skilled and cunning player. He seemed to be able to do anything with the ball short of making it speak! Maradona carried the Argentine team on his back at the 1986 World Cup, all the way to the finals against the fierce West German team, where he took on every role. He scored a total of five goals in the competition and set up five more. Though he did not manage to score in the finals, he provided the assist that secured victory for his team.

DIEGO MARADONA
B. 1960
National games, 1977–1991: 91
Goals: 34

GOLD MEDAL AT 1986 WORLD CUP
Final, June 29
Mexico City, Mexico

ARGENTINA – WEST GERMANY
3-2

Brown 23'	Rummenigge 74'
Valdano 56'	Völler 81'
Burruchaga 84'	

Nery Pumpido, goalkeeper
Ruggeri – Brown – Cuciuffo – Olarticoechea
Giusti – Burruchaga (Trobbiani +90') – Batista – Enrique
Valdano – Maradona

Coach Carlos Bilardo

"THE HAND OF GOD"

Maradona had a magnificent play—known as the "Goal of the Century"—in a game against England at the 1986 World Cup: He ran half the length of the field, shook off a number of defenders, and finally blasted the ball into the net. A goal he made earlier in that game is even more famous, in which he deliberately—and illegally—used his hand to thrust the ball into the net. The referee failed to notice what had taken place and allowed the goal. Afterwards Maradona claimed, with a smirk, that "the hand of God" had been responsible for the goal.

19

NEW MASTER

Maradona's performance during the 1986 World Cup was so brilliant that the Argentines did not dare to dream of ever acquiring a similar legendary player. However, only 360 days after the final game, an heir was born!

When Messi was a boy his grandmother used to take care of him while his parents were at work. She would often take his older brothers to soccer practice, and Messi would tag along. He had just started playing with the ball at home and was obviously talented and passionate. However, he was rather short for his age and not very powerfully built.

One day one of the teams was missing one player. It's not clear whether it was the coach or Messi's grandmother who suggested that little Messi should play with the older boys, but he was led to the field. He was shy and timid but wanted to play with the ball.

Messi's grandmother and the coach decided that it would be best to have him play along the sideline so it would be easy to call him off the field if the older boys hurt him and made him cry.

The first time the ball passed to Messi nothing happened. He caught the ball with his right foot and didn't know what to do with it. The ball just bounced away. But the next time he caught the ball with his left foot and the little guy took off.

Messi surged down the field with the ball and when one of the big boys came running to take the ball off him, little Messi dodged him easily.

The coach figured he got lucky and yelled at Messi to pass the ball. But the boy just kept on running, taking on one player after another. None of them managed to get the ball off him. His grandmother and the coach watched in awe. They both knew that they'd witnessed the birth of a new genius.

At the age of five Messi started to play with a small club coached by his dad in Rosario called Grandoli. Soccer fever ran deep within the close-knit Messi family. Soon stories of the talented youngster spread and in 1995 he was training with Newell's Old Boys, the largest club in Rosario.

Everyone could see that the boy had great potential. The trouble was that he didn't seem to grow normally and was by far the smallest boy his age. It turned out that he suffered from growth-hormone deficiency. Chances were that he would always be very short—and obviously far too small to make it to the very top.

The solution was to give Messi daily hormone injections. He didn't enjoy it but he bit the bullet and from the age of nine Messi could give himself the injections. He started to grow again but the shots were expensive and the Messi family didn't have the means to pay for them. Newell's Old Boys covered the costs.

In 2000 Argentina suffered a bad financial crash, similar to the one that would hit globally in 2008. Money disappeared; everyone had to cut back on spending. Newell's Old Boys could no longer afford to pay for Messi's hormone injections. The boy was thirteen years old and still very small for his age. He would likely never grow to his full height.

Messi was very fond of his grandmother Celia, who used to take him to his first soccer practices. He was devastated when she died in 1998. He honors her memory by raising his finger to the sky after scoring a goal.

TWO GREAT TALENTS

Incredibly enough, Messi's childhood coaches insist that there was another boy in the same school who matched him in skill and potential. He was called Gustavo but was not as fortunate as Messi, who came from a loving and supportive family. The boys both lived in poor neighborhoods in Rosario, and some young people turned to crime, drinking, able to give him the support he needed to develop his talents. Bit by bit he lost his way and finally succumbed to alcohol and drugs, his talent wasted and gone. The two boys thus have very different stories. Lionel Messi had a caring family that supported him in every way possible, and he became the greatest soccer player in the world. Gustavo, however, is

BARCELONA!

The future didn't look too good for Lionel Messi. It seemed like he would have to quit his hormone treatment, which in turn meant he would remain quite small and never manage to reach the top league of soccer players. He had little interest in anything else; he was but an average student, although he did show some artistic talent.

But suddenly events took an unexpected turn. Two men who had read reports in the local papers in Rosario on the young—but short—genius came to see the family. They had been in contact with the great Spanish soccer club FC Barcelona and said they could arrange for Messi to have a trial with the team.

If Messi could get a contract with

Barcelona, the club would foot his medical bills so he could reach a normal height. It also meant he would be able to do what he was clearly meant to do—play soccer.

Messi's father flew with his son to Spain where he trained for a week with the club's junior team in September 2000. Anyone could see that the boy was almost ridiculously talented, but did it make sense to bet on a little kid from Argentina, not knowing how he would grow and mature?

Carles Rexach

The coaches of the junior and cadet teams could not reach a decision. They waited for Carles Rexach to return. He was the manager of the club and was abroad that first week when the Messis were in town.

When Rexach returned Messi was playing in a game. Rexach

Without hormone injections 4' 8"

Carles Rexach

Messi's first FC Barcelona ID card

With hormone injections 5' 7"

watched in awe as he walked around the field to where the coaches sat. "It took me seven minutes," he later said. "And when I sat down on that bench I had made my decision. I said to the coaches: *We have to sign him. Now.* For what did I see? A kid who was very small, but totally different from anyone else. He had incredible confidence, agility, speed, great technique; he could run full speed with the ball, dodging anyone in his way without hesitation. It wasn't difficult to spot; these talents everyone now knows were obvious, even though he was just thirteen years old.

Some soccer players need a good team to flourish, but not Messi. People sometimes say that I discovered Messi, but that's nonsense. His talents were there for all to see. If a Martian who'd never seen a game of soccer would have watched Messi play, he would still have understood that this kid was one of a kind."

Everyone seemed happy. Jorge Messi and Lionel went back to Argentina, and the family started to prepare to move to Barcelona. It was clear that they would not go unless everyone in the family agreed. The three boys now had a sister named Marisol, who had been born in 1995. Everyone was on board; this was a chance of a lifetime for the Little Lion and they had to take it.

A Contract on a Napkin

After a few months, Messi's agents were growing restless waiting for the contract. They went to Rexach and told him to get the papers in order, because Real Madrid was showing interest in the young Messi, and they were ready to start negotiations. Rexach didn't hesitate: he grabbed the next piece of paper he got his hands on, a paper napkin. He drew up a contract on the napkin and signed it. And that was how Lionel Messi, at the tender age of thirteen, was signed to FC Barcelona. In February 2001 the whole Messi family arrived in Barcelona, and Lionel started training with his new teammates.

In 1899 a young immigrant from Switzerland settled in Barcelona. His name was Joan Gamper and he had learned to play soccer in his native country. He took out an ad in the paper asking if there were any young men who would like to join him in establishing a soccer team. Eleven people showed up, and Futbol Club Barcelona was born.

The club gradually became a force to be reckoned with. The Spanish Championship, La Liga, was founded in 1929. Barça won the championship, Real Madrid ending up in second place.

These two clubs have since been dominant in Spanish soccer. From 1953 to 1969 Real Madrid reigned supreme, claiming the title 11 times in this 16-year period. Spain's dictator, Francisco Franco, was a fan of the club, and it acquired many of the strongest players in the world.

But Barça was never far behind, and during the season of 1990–1991 the team took off. The coach was Dutchman Johan Cruyff, who assembled the so-called Dream Team that won La Liga for four consecutive seasons. Another Dutchman, Louis van Gaal, brought home the title twice just before 2000, but then the club hit a slump and didn't win any titles for five years.

In 2003 the club hired yet another Dutchman, Frank Rijkaard, in the hopes of turning things around. And it worked; Barcelona won two championship titles and beat Arsenal 2–1 in the European Champions League final in 2005–2006. But then Barça seemed to lose focus, and Rijkaard left in 2008.

The next coach was a former Barcelona player who had been coaching Barcelona's junior team. With Pep Guardiola the club rose to great heights. He developed even further the impressive passing game that had become Barcelona's specialty. And into the pivotal role of forward he moved his best player: Lionel Messi.

THE TRI

CATALONIA

Barcelona is the capital city of a region in Spain called Catalonia. Catalans have their own language—Catalan—that is closely related to Spanish (Castilian). Catalans are very proud of their identity and like to keep the government in Madrid at an arm's length. Catalonia covers an area that is slightly larger than Belgium. It has a population of 7.5 million; roughly 2 million live in the capital, Barcelona.

PORTUGAL

FRANCE

Catalonia

Barcelona

Madrid

Mallorca

The Mediterranean

UMPHANT BARÇA

Messi celebrating with his teammates, just one of the guys. Can you spot him? In spite of his tremendous individual skill, he always stresses that soccer is a team sport!

25

The old farmhouse
La Masia is right beside
Barça's stadium, Camp Nou.

THE FLEA OF LA MASIA

It was clear that the young Lionel Messi was in the right place as soon as he came to Barcelona. No other club takes as excellent care of its younger teams as Barça does.

Since 1979, the club's soon-to-be celebrated youth academy has been based in a 300-year-old country house by Camp Nou called La Masia or "the farm."

For the past 30 years Barça has focused on rearing homegrown virtuosos rather than simply buying skilled players from other clubs.

Pep Guardiola is one of many players who went through the La Masia soccer school. He was FC Barcelona's main midfielder from 1990 to 2001, and then became a coach with the club, at first with the junior teams and then with the senior team.

La Masia emphasizes pinpoint-accurate passes and collaboration between teammates. Everyone has to work together. This is how Barcelona manages its incredible ball possession during games. The passes tend to be unbelievably accurate, and sometimes the team can keep the ball for great lengths of time until someone finds a gap in the opposing team's defense. And then, in a second, the defense is ripped open with magnificent play.

This is what Barcelona players learn in La Masia. It's usually called "tiki-taka." This sort of game suits a skilled player like Messi perfectly. Few players are as good at keeping the ball as he is.

Even though he was growing normally again, Messi was still rather short and was often called La Pulga, or "The Flea." Alongside Messi, there were other youngsters of the same age in La Masia, such as the defender Gerard Piqué and the midfielder Cesc Fàbregas. The three of them played together for a few seasons, until Piqué was transferred to Manchester United and Fàbregas to Arsenal.

Messi stayed with Barça and kept on sharpening his skills and maturing as a player in La Masia. Fàbregas and Piqué are now back in Barcelona and the trio now plays together once again.

BREAKING RECORDS

After Ronaldinho left Barcelona, the club revolved around the trio of Messi, Xavi, and Iniesta. It is almost unprecedented for a single soccer team to be able to boast of having three such legends in their ranks at the same time!

Barcelona's captain, Charles Puyol, and his players celebrate the young Messi's first goal against Albacete. Messi is embraced by Mexican defensive stalwart Rafael Márquez.

Lionel Messi soon made a name for himself with Barcelona's Juvenil and Cadet teams. The hormone treatments were successful, and he was growing and gaining strength. Frank Rijkaard, who took over as coach in 2003, believed in the young Argentine. Messi had proved to be quite the goalscorer and in November 2003 he debuted with Barcelona's first team in a friendly match against Porto. He was 16 years old.

On October 16, 2004, Messi debuted in La Liga with Barça's first team. It was a game against Espanyol, the city's second largest club. Messi was 17 years old and was the youngest player to play for Barça in La Liga. He played several games with the team during that season and on December 7 he played his first game in the European Champions League. It was in the city of Donetsk in Ukraine, and Barça lost to the home team, Shakthar.

On May 1, 2005, Messi scored his first goal for Barcelona's senior team. The club was playing Albacete in Camp Nou. He came in for Samuel Eto'o, who was Barça's reigning scorer at the time.

Messi had a great connection with the Brazilian genius Ronaldinho, who was in Barça's front line. Shortly after Messi came into the game he flipped the ball over Albacete's goalkeeper after an assist from Ronaldinho. The referee claimed he was offside and wouldn't count the goal as valid, which was a questionable call.

But Ronaldinho and Messi simply repeated the feat, and Messi scored his first valid senior goal in injury time. He was the youngest player to score for the club. Both Barça players and fans went wild, because everyone could sense that this was a historic moment in Camp Nou.

MESSI SPEAKS

I HAVE FUN, LIKE A KID PLAYING SOCCER IN THE STREET. IF THE DAY COMES WHEN I STOP HAVING FUN, I AM GOING TO QUIT.

BEING NOMINATED THE BEST IN SOMETHING IS BEAUTIFUL AND SPECIAL. BUT IF THERE ARE NO TITLES, YOU HAVEN'T WON ANYTHING.

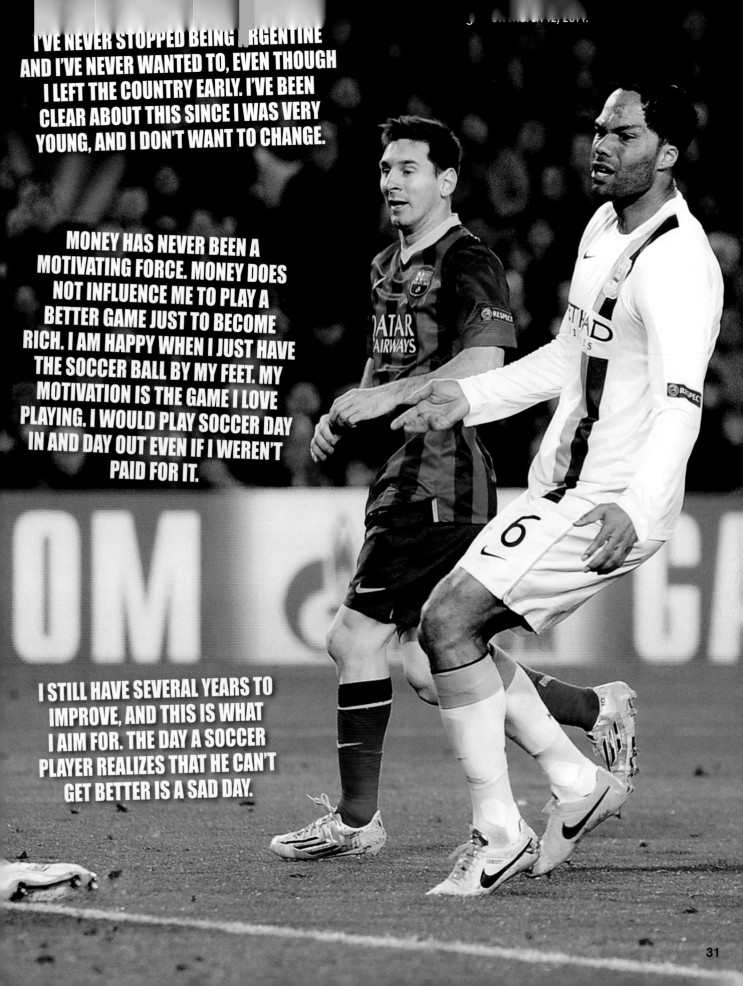

I'VE NEVER STOPPED BEING ARGENTINE AND I'VE NEVER WANTED TO, EVEN THOUGH I LEFT THE COUNTRY EARLY. I'VE BEEN CLEAR ABOUT THIS SINCE I WAS VERY YOUNG, AND I DON'T WANT TO CHANGE.

MONEY HAS NEVER BEEN A MOTIVATING FORCE. MONEY DOES NOT INFLUENCE ME TO PLAY A BETTER GAME JUST TO BECOME RICH. I AM HAPPY WHEN I JUST HAVE THE SOCCER BALL BY MY FEET. MY MOTIVATION IS THE GAME I LOVE PLAYING. I WOULD PLAY SOCCER DAY IN AND DAY OUT EVEN IF I WEREN'T PAID FOR IT.

I STILL HAVE SEVERAL YEARS TO IMPROVE, AND THIS IS WHAT I AIM FOR. THE DAY A SOCCER PLAYER REALIZES THAT HE CAN'T GET BETTER IS A SAD DAY.

AN EPIC GOAL!

5 SHOT AND GOAL

4 FOILS THE KEEPER

3 DRIVES ON BETWEEN DEFENDERS

2 TEARS UP THE FIELD

1 SLIPS BY TWO DEFENDERS

3

When Messi takes off with the ball he is almost unstoppable. No other player today can match his ball control. It's worth noting that however many defenders hassle him and try to tackle him, legally or illegally, Messi never takes a dive. He always tries to stay on his feet and keep going. That's where his wizardry comes from.

SCAN THE CODE AND SEE THE PLAY!

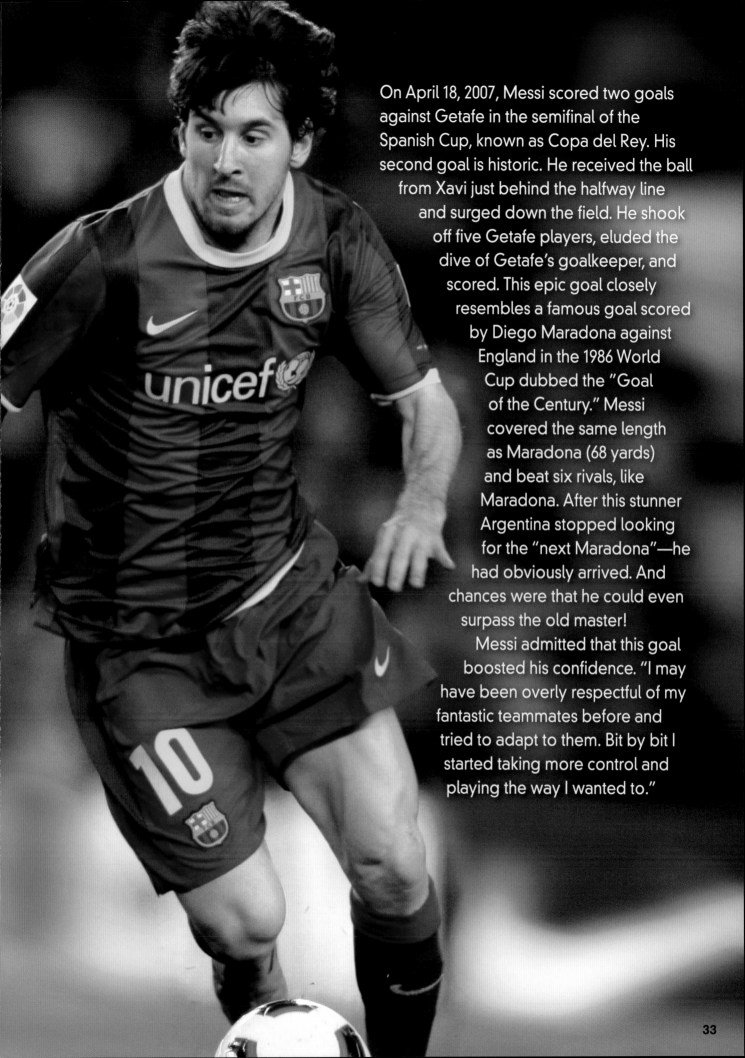

On April 18, 2007, Messi scored two goals against Getafe in the semifinal of the Spanish Cup, known as Copa del Rey. His second goal is historic. He received the ball from Xavi just behind the halfway line and surged down the field. He shook off five Getafe players, eluded the dive of Getafe's goalkeeper, and scored. This epic goal closely resembles a famous goal scored by Diego Maradona against England in the 1986 World Cup dubbed the "Goal of the Century." Messi covered the same length as Maradona (68 yards) and beat six rivals, like Maradona. After this stunner Argentina stopped looking for the "next Maradona"—he had obviously arrived. And chances were that he could even surpass the old master!

Messi admitted that this goal boosted his confidence. "I may have been overly respectful of my fantastic teammates before and tried to adapt to them. Bit by bit I started taking more control and playing the way I wanted to."

Guido Buchwald, a player for West Germany (left), trips Diego Maradona during the 1990 World Cup final between Argentina and West Germany. Lothar Mattäus (right) also has the Argentine genius in his sights.

They have scored the most for Argentina

Place	Player	Years	Games	Goals
1	Batistuta	1991–2002	78	56
2	Messi	2005–	83	37
3	Crespo	1995–2007	64	35
4	Maradona	1977–1994	91	34

LACKING THE CLINCHER

After becoming World Cup champions in 1978 and 1986, the Argentines had tasted success and they craved nothing more than winning the title for a third time. At the 1990 World Cup, held in Italy, the team once again faced the Germans in the final game. This time, however, they lost, in a tedious match full of hostility and ugly plays. Maradona had been in trouble with illegal drugs and the law and seemed to be in bad health. The Argentines were sad to see the downfall of their hero, but eventually Maradona succeeded in overcoming most of his problems. In the following years, the national team continued playing fantastic soccer. In fact, skilled and daring soccer players seemed to sprout up all over the country in the wake of Maradona. In the last decade of the 20th century and the first of the new millennium, Argentina acquired a host of great individuals who often played fantastically together as a team. Unfortunately, the teams appeared tragically fragile and despite advancing in one World Cup competition after the other, Argentina kept losing the decisive games. It seemed as if they always lacked the clincher—that winning touch that would seal the deal.

But around the middle of the first decade of the century, the Argentines got wind of a young compatriot living in Spain who they believed could make a difference.

Gabriel Omar Batistuta racked up goals for Argentina from 1991 to 2002. Batistuta won the Copa América title in 1991 and 1993. He remains the top goalscorer for the Argentine national team, scoring 56 goals in 78 games!

YOUNGEST PLAYER IN THE WORLD CUP

In 2004 Lionel Messi was invited to play for the Spanish national U-20 team, for which he was eligible since he moved to Spain at the age of 13. Messi declined the offer because he wanted to play only for Argentina.

In the summer of 2005 Messi led the Argentine U-20 team to victory in the FIFA World Youth Championship. He was the top scorer in the tournament and was awarded both the Golden Ball and the Golden Shoe. Yet he was one of the two youngest players on the squad. Only Sergio Agüero was younger than Messi. Later that summer Messi made his full international debut in a friendly game against Hungary on August 17, 2005. He had just turned 18 but was already famous for his extraordinary skills, so expectations were high when he came on during the 63rd minute.

But he did not stay long. He got the ball immediately and dribbled easily past a Hungarian defender, who was not about to let the young genius leave him in the dust—and tugged at Messi's shirt. Messi batted out an arm to free himself, and his arm landed on the chest or neck of the defender, who then took a dive, acting as if Messi had elbowed him in the face. Unfortunately the referee fell for it and sent Messi off after roughly 60 seconds on the field.

Fortunately his coach, José Pekerman, supported Messi, and the young man tried to take it on the chin. But back in the locker room Messi broke down in tears, the disappointment was so great.

Two weeks later Messi played his first proper international with the senior team when Argentina took on Paraguay in the 2006 World Cup qualifier. In October he was on the senior team and at the age of 18 he played with Argentine greats such as Hernán Crespo and Juan Ramán Riquelme.

When the Argentine national team was preparing for the 2006 World Cup Messi scored his first international goal. He scored against Croatia in a friendly match on March 1. He then joined the team in Germany for the World Cup. He came on as a substitute in a match against Serbia on June 16, 2006, and scored his first goal in a major international tournament minutes later, the final goal in Argentina's 6–0 victory. He was only 18—the youngest Argentine to represent his country at a World Cup. Even Maradona

Messi in a match with Argentina
against Holland in 2006

DISAPPOINTMENT AT THE COPA

The championship of South America is called the Copa América. Lionel Messi competed for the first time in the Copa in the summer of 2007. Argentina played brilliantly, with Riquelme running the show and Crespo, Messi, and Carlos Tévez forming a formidable front line. The team won its first five games and raked in the goals. The magic unexpectedly wore off in the final when the Argentine team broke down and lost 3–0 to an opportunistic Brazil. Messi scored two goals in the Copa 2007 and was voted Best Young Player.

was older than Messi when he debuted in the World Cup in 1982.

Argentina played very well to begin with but lost to Germany in a penalty shootout in the quarterfinal. Pekerman left Messi on the bench for that match, though he probably shouldn't have.

There were many young promising players debuting in the World Cup of 2006. In addition to Messi there were

Cristiano Ronaldo from Portugal, Wayne Rooney from England, Robin van Persie from the Netherlands, and Fernando Torres from Spain. None of them was awarded the Best Young Player—that honor went to Lukas Podolski from Germany.

Italy was the dark horse of the tournament and became the unexpected world champion.

EVEN THE MIGHTY FALL

Argentina was off to a bad start in the 2010 World Cup qualifying process, and for a while it seemed like the squad would not make it to the finals in South Africa. Much to everyone's surprise, Diego Maradona was asked to take over as coach. He had been the best soccer player in the world and was greatly loved in Argentina. But he had little experience as a coach and there were ups and downs. Maradona had trouble getting Messi and the other brilliant forwards in the squad going. They almost didn't qualify for the tournament. Messi scored only four goals in the qualification stage, which totaled 18 games.

Once in South Africa, however, Argentina and Messi played well, winning all their games at the group stage, and beating Mexico in the Round of 16. Their front line was lethal, with Gonzalo Higuaín and Tévez at the front, Messi right behind them, and Agüero on the substitute bench. Messi didn't score but he was a great playmaker. The World Cup title seemed a very real possibility.

Then disaster struck. In the quarterfinal the Argentine team crumbled when faced with the Germans, and lost 4–0. It was their biggest loss in the World Cup since 1974. The sting was especially painful because they had the two geniuses, Messi and Maradona, at the helm. Two

of the very best in history! But there it is. Argentina was out.

Maradona was fired. Spain won the title. The Argentines got a chance to patch up their wounded pride a couple of months later when the recently crowned world champions paid them a visit. Spain and Argentina played a friendly match in Buenos Aires, and the Argentines crushed the Spaniards in a 4–1 victory. Messi scored the first of his team's four goals. If only this had been the World Cup final!

Creative

Messi was nominated for the FIFA Golden Ball award in the 2010 World Cup, despite failing to score a goal in the tournament. He was judged to be: "Outstanding in his pace and creativity for his team, dribbling, shooting, passing—spectacular and efficient."

Another Copa Disappointment

Messi's fourth attempt to win a major tournament with the Argentine national team was unsuccessful in the 2011 Copa América. The team did not perform to standard and was eliminated in the quarterfinals after a penalty shootout against Uruguay. Messi did not manage to score a goal in the tournament. He has yet to score a goal in the finals of a major international tournament since 2007.

At the end of March 2014, Messi had played 83 internationals and scored 37 goals.

Maradona consoles Messi after a devastating World Cup loss to the Germans on July 3, 2010.

AN AMAZING RUN FOR BARCELONA

Even though the going was often tough with the Argentina national team, Messi was always successful with Barcelona. The young player, who because of his size and shyness was not expected to amount to much, was already scoring more goals each season than many other soccer players would be proud to score in an entire career.

2004–2005 La Liga

1	Barcelona	84
2	Real Madrid	80
3	Villarreal	65

Messi 1 goal

UEFA Champions League: Barcelona lost in the Round of 16 to Chelsea. Liverpool claimed the title. Messi did not score in the CL campaign.

Messi scored 1 goal during the season.

2005–2006 La Liga

1	Barcelona	82
2	Real Madrid	70
3	Valencia	69

Messi 6 goals

UEFA Champions League: Barcelona beat Arsenal in the final to claim the title. Messi scored 1 goal.

Messi scored a total of 8 goals during the season.

2006–2007 La Liga

1	Real Madrid	76
2	Barcelona	76
3	Sevilla	71

Messi 14 goals

UEFA Champions League: Barcelona lost in the Round of 16 to Liverpool. AC Milan claimed the title. Messi scored 1 goal.

Messi scored a total of 17 goals during the season.

2007–2008 La Liga

1	Real Madrid	85
2	Villarreal	77
3	Barcelona	67

Messi 10 goals

UEFA Champions League: Barcelona lost in the semifinals to Manchester United, who went on to win the title. Messi scored 6 goals.

Messi scored a total of 16 goals during the season.

2008–2009 La Liga

1	Barcelona	87
2	Real Madrid	78
3	Sevilla	70

Messi 23 goals

UEFA Champions League: Barcelona beat Manchester United in the final. Messi scored 9 goals.
Top scorer!

Messi scored a total of 38 goals during the season.

2009–2010 La Liga

1	Barcelona	99
2	Real Madrid	96
3	Valencia	71

Messi 34 goals
Top scorer!

UEFA Champions League: Barcelona lost in the semifinals to Inter Milan, who went on to claim the title. Messi scored 8 goals.
Top scorer!

Messi scored a total of 47 goals during the season.

2010–2011 La Liga

1	Barcelona	96
2	Real Madrid	92
3	Valencia	71

UEFA Champions League: Barcelona beat Manchester United in the final. Messi scored 12 goals.
Top scorer!

Messi scored a total of 53 goals during the season.

2011–2012 La Liga

1	Real Madrid	100
2	Barcelona	91
3	Valencia	61

Messi 50 goals
Top scorer!

UEFA Champions League: Barcelona lost in the semifinals to Chelsea, who went on to claim the title. Messi scored 14 goals.
Top scorer!

Messi scored a total of 72 goals during the season.

2012–2013 La Liga

1	Barcelona	100
2	Real Madrid	85
3	Atlético Madrid	76

Messi 46 goals
Top scorer!

UEFA Champions League: Barcelona crashed in the semifinals against Bayern Munich, which went on to win the title. Messi scored 8 goals.

Messi scored a total of 60 goals during

THE GOLDEN BOY!

The most prestigious award offered to soccer players is called the Ballon d'Or, or the Golden Ball. Three players had won this award three times apiece before Messi entered the scene: the Dutchmen Johan Cruyff and Marco Van Basten and the Frenchman Michel Platini. Messi, however, made history when he won the Golden Ball for the *fourth* consecutive time in 2012. Yet another win is not unlikely, but an injury in 2013 prevented it from happening that year. This much, however, is true: Messi has not grown tired of playing for the gold!

Messi with his four Golden Balls!

FIFA
BALLON
D'OR

Messi is not only daring on the soccer field—
many people thought he was also very daring
when he accepted the fourth Golden Ball
wearing this dashing suit!

43

91 GOALS

In 1972, Gerd Müller, a forward with Bayern Munich and the German national team, made 85 goals in 60 games. Few believed that this record would ever be beaten by a player in a powerful league. However, Messi beat the record in 2012. He scored 91 goals in 69 games.

Gerd Müller

IN ONE YEAR!

MESSI BEAT MOST WORLDWIDE GOAL-SCORING RECORDS IN TH[E] FANTASTIC YEAR OF 2012.

Messi's Goals

Tournament	Games	Goals
La Liga	38	59
Copa del Rey	8	5
Spanish Super Cup	2	2
UEFA Champions League	12	13
National Team	9	12
	69	**91**

Nineteen of these goals were pe[nalty] kicks. Messi missed only one penalty during that year, in a g[ame] against Chelsea. Chelsea mad[e] it to the finals of the U[EFA] Champions Leag[ue].

In that year, Mes[si] failed to make a [goal] in 22 games, but scored two goals [in] an equal number [of] games.

Messi achieved ni[ne] hat tricks. In additi[on,] twice scored four [goals] in a single game [and] once five. He ma[de] goals from insid[e the] penalty box an[d] outside it.

During the 2011-[12] season, Messi s[cored 73] goals, which st[ands as a] European reco[rd.]

MESSI'S STRENGTHS

Matches between Barcelona and Real Madrid are called "El Clásico." For one of these pivotal matches the BBC asked striker Eidur Gudjohnsen to compare the two star players on the rival teams, Cristiano Ronaldo and LIONEL MESSI.

Gudjohnsen knows both players well, having faced Ronaldo several times when he was with Chelsea, and having been Messi's teammate in Barça for three years—just when Messi was emerging on the scene. See what Gudjohnsen had to say about Messi and how he rated him on various levels.

Technique

The BBC journalist said that Messi's feet are "as sensitive as a pickpocket's hands." He went on to say that no other player has shown that level of ball control. "His bewildering repertoire of feints and swerves, sudden stops and demoralizing spurts leave defenders dumbfounded time and again."

Gudjohnsen: "His control is the best I have ever seen, it is truly breathtaking."

10/10

Heading Ability

Despite his height Messi has scored some memorable headers. Who can forget the second goal in the Champions League 2009 final in Rome when he sealed the victory for Barça against ManU?

Gudjohnsen: "His size is not a problem. You can't afford to underestimate him in the air; if you do, he will find the net."

6/10

Free Kicks

Messi is a good shooter and is capable of exquisite free-kick

goals, though he maybe has yet to match his rival's great variations of free kicks.

Gudjohnsen: "He has so much ability and such magic in his feet that he can do anything with a dead ball."

7/10

Team Player

Messi is the ultimate team player and a great part of his success comes down to the beautiful team play between him and the likes of Xavi and Iniesta. He seems to almost read his teammates' minds and selflessly drags defenders away with runs to free up his mates.

Gudjohnsen: "He is the perfect teammate. Quiet, dignified, brilliant to play with."

9/10

Goals

Messi and Ronaldo are the greatest goalscorers of today and possibly of all time. They are both incredible soccer players, but the diminutive Argentine unquestionably has that something extra special that we have never seen before.

Gudjohnsen: "It's so hard to say one is better than the other. They are reaching standards that very few of us have seen anyone reach in recent years. But Messi narrowly has the edge. I have never seen anything like him. We'd be lucky to be watching one of them. To be entertained by both is a blessing."

10/10

Messi and Gudjohnsen celebrating Messi's goal against Almeria at Camp Nou in October 2007.

FAVORITES

Favorite Food:
Milanesa à la Napolitana

essi loves traditional Argentine food
oked by his parents.

A strong favorite is *Milanesa à la
apolitana* or Neapolitan-style schnitzel.
essi's mother, Celia, cooks it something
e this:

he takes slices of beef, thins them with
eat-hammer, sprinkles on salt, dips
m into whisked eggs, and covers them
readcrumbs.

he then fries them in a shallow pan
l they are a lovely golden brown and
es them into an oven.

hile the schnitzel is in the oven, Celia
sliced onions until they soften and

turn yellow, then she adds chopped
tomatoes, a bit of water, salt, dried
oregano, and a pinch of sugar. She
allows this to simmer for 20 minutes, and
then the mixture is poured over the meat.
She takes care to cover it completely.

The whole thing is topped off with
slices of cheese, or even cream cheese,
before it is returned back into the oven.
While the cheese melts, Celia fries some
potatoes, which she serves with the
schnitzel.

Messi gobbles this up with delight! And
it must be good for you, otherwise such a
healthy sports hero would hardly eat it!

FAVORITE DESSERT:
Dulce de leche: pudding made by slowly simmering milk and sugar, reminiscent of runny caramel.

FAVORITE MOVIES:
There are two: *Son of the Bride*— a dramatic comedy about a man and his mother, who suffers from Alzheimer's. This movie reminds Messi of his beloved grandmother, who suffered a similar illness. The other movie is called *Nine Queens* and is a clever crime story about two con artists. Both movies star Ricardo Darín, one Argentina's most popular movie stars.

FAVORITE BOOK:
Diego Maradona's biography. Messi has yet to finish it, and he owns up to being a lazy reader. Sometimes he does, however, mention a long epic poem from Argentina called *El Martín Fierro* that describes an almost "Wild West" atmosphere in Argentina in the 19th century.

FAVORITE MUSIC:
Argentine *cumbia* music: fast and passionate South American dance music. Find it on YouTube!

SUPERSTITION:
Messi will not admit to any superstitions but he insists on playing with wet hair.

WHAT HE HATES:
Injustice and ill treatment of the poor.

Messi and Antonella Roccuzzo have been a couple since 2009. Like Messi, she is from Rosario in Argentina. Their parents are friends, and they first met when they were five years old. When Messi returned home for Christmas 2009, he and Antonella saw each other for the first time in several years, and love blossomed between them. Their son, Thiago, was born in November 2012.

Neymar with his son David Lucca and teammate Messi with his son Thiago pose for a photo prior to a game, September 2013 in Barcelona, Spain.

CHANGING TIMES

THERE HAVE BEEN MANY CHANGES IN MESSI'S LIFE, BOTH PERSONALLY AND PROFESSIONALLY.

Messi has not only gained a child, he has also gained new companions on the front lines in Barcelona. Neymar, born in 1992 in Brazil, joined the Barça team in the summer of 2013, and many expect that in time he will become one of the world's greatest soccer players. Neymar and Messi immediately formed a close relationship, both on the field and off. Pictured here are Messi and Neymar with their sons. Neymar had his son, David Lucca, when he was only 19 years old.

Despite the friendship between Messi and Neymar, they played on rival national teams in the 2014 World Cup!

10 FACTS

A familiar sight. Defenders gather around Messi.

An even more familiar sight, Messi about to shoot.

When Messi scored 73 goals in the 2011–2012 season he set a world record of most scored goals in one season. The previous record holder was the Scotsman Archie Stark, who scored 70 goals for a U.S. club in the 1920s.

When Ronaldinho left Barça in 2008, Messi inherited his number 10 shirt. Ever since the Brazilian genius Pelé was assigned the number, it has been worn by creative playmakers, attacking midfielders, or even "second strikers." Maradona always wore the number 10, and now Messi also wears the shirt with the Argentine national team.

Messi signed a contract with the Chinese automobile company Chery to promote the luxury vehicle Riich G5. His favorite sports car, however, is the Ferrari Spyder.

His full name is Lionel Andrés Messi.

During his first seasons with Barcelona Messi was prone to injuries and had to rest for weeks on end. The club's doctors believed that growth spurts due to the hormone treatments were to blame. They developed a series of stretches for him to do, and since then Messi has suffered very few injuries.

Messi's parents, Jorge and Celia, once considered moving to Australia, where they had a better chance of employment than back home in Argentina. Messi was not born at that time. But what would have become of Leo Messi in Australia?

Messi played with the Argentine national team at the 2008 Beijing Olympics. The team won all its matches and beat Nigeria 1–0 in the final. Ángel Di María scored the winning goal after an assist from Messi, who scored two goals in the games.

Zlatan Ibrahimović was Messi's teammate at Barça for one season. He did not live up to expectations in Barcelona but he has great respect for Messi. When asked who was better, Messi or Ronaldo, Zlatan answered: "Messi is a natural. Ronaldo is the result of training."

When Messi arrived in Barcelona at the age of 13 to try out for the Barça management, his father promised him a

Argentina national team members ranked by most games played:

Rank	Name	Years	Goals	Games
1	Zanetti	1994–2011	5	145
2	Ayala	1994–2007	7	115
3	Simone	1988–2002	11	106
3	Mascherano	2003–	3	106
5	Ruggeri	1983–1994	7	97
6	Messi	2005–	42	93
7	Maradona	1977–1994	34	91
8	Ortega	1993–2010	17	87
9	Batistuta	1991–2002	56	78
10	Sorín	1996–2006	11	76

new track suit if he scored six goals in the first trial game. Messi scored five but got the track suit anyway, as his sixth, an offside goal, was disallowed.

Maradona

The first time Messi met Diego Maradona he wanted to ask his idol for an autograph or to have their picture taken together. When he faced Maradona he became so shy that he couldn't utter a word and didn't dare ask for anything.

Zlatan celebrates with his teammates in Barcelona.

HOW TALL IS HE?

Messi is living proof that size doesn't matter. And not just Messi: Some of Barcelona's other greats are also on the shorter side. Xavi, Iniesta, and Pedro are all 5'7"— the same height as their teammate Messi.

HEIGHT UNDER THE BAR: 8 FEET

LIONEL
MESSI
5'7"

CRISTIANO
RONALDO
6'1"

NEYMAR
5'9"

DIEGO
MARADONA
5'5"

MORE RECORDS!

Messi continues to break records. On March 23, 2014, Messi scored a hat trick in a great game held at Santiago Bernabéu Stadium in the Spanish capital when Barcelona beat Real Madrid 4–3. At this, Messi became all-time top goalscorer in matches between Barça and Real. He scored 21 goals in 27 games against Real.

Alfredo Di Stéfano was the previous record holder. Stéfano scored 18 goals in 30 games from 1953–1964. Next comes Raúl (Real) with 15; then César Rodriguez (Barcelona); then Puskás and Gento from Madrid. Cristiano Ronaldo is in 7th place on this list with 13 goals in 21 Clásico games.

With the same hat trick, Messi knocked Hugo Sánchez from his position as the top goalscorer in La Liga. Messi had scored 236 goals in 268 games. There is little doubt that Messi will eventually reach the top. The top position belongs to Telmo Zarra with no less than 252 goals in 277 games from 1940–1955.

GARETH BALE 6'

LUIS SUÁREZ 5'11"

ZLATAN IBRAHIMOVIĆ 6'5"

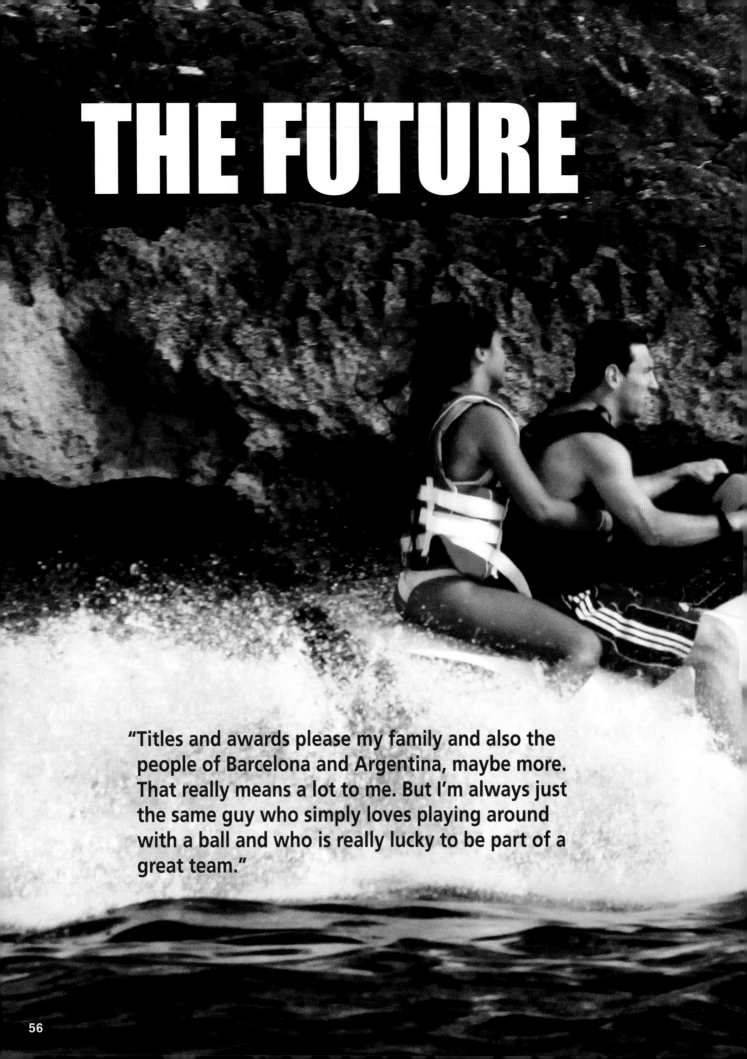

THE FUTURE

"Titles and awards please my family and also the people of Barcelona and Argentina, maybe more. That really means a lot to me. But I'm always just the same guy who simply loves playing around with a ball and who is really lucky to be part of a great team."

Lionel Messi has a humble and quiet demeanor despite always rushing onward and upward.

Messi turned 27 years old as the 2014 World Cup was at its peak. He put all his effort into the position as team captain at the 2014 World Cup!

Messi has already had such incredible success with Barcelona that it is hard to imagine how he can progess further. But he claims that he is far from becoming tired of the beautiful game. He also insists that he has no desire to play for another club and would prefer to spend his entire career with Barcelona.

There is no doubt that he still has more to offer the Argentine national team, and his biggest dream is to lift the World Cup. He wants to bring home the trophy to please his fellow countrymen of Argentina.

When he retires he intends to move back home to Rosario and live surrounded by his loved ones.

In the summer of 2013 the hugely promising Brazilian forward Neymar joined Barcelona. He claimed his main objective was to help Messi become an even better player. For soccer fans their cooperation on the field is a mouth-watering prospect.

ARGENTINA NOW

THE GOALKEEPER

Sergo Romero was born in 1987. Romero was first chosen for the national team in 2009 by Maradona and has kept his position ever since. Romero plays with the French team Monaco but is not a regular member of the team. Sabella has however remained faithful to him in the national team.

DEFENDER

Pablo Zabaleta is the most famous of the defenders. He is a right back with Manchester City. Other players include Fernández with Napoli, Fabricio Coloccini with Newcastle, and Marcos Rojo, Ezequiel Garay, and Nicolás Otamendi, who all play in Portugal.

THE FIGHTER

Javier Mascherano was born in 1984. He played with River Plate in Buenos Aires and later with Corinthians in Brazil and West Ham in England. In 2007 Mascherano was transferred to Liverpool and he has played with Barcelona since 2010. Mascherano is a hot-tempered fighter on midfield but he can also play

defense. First and foremost, Mascherano has the role of crushing the offense of the opponents. He unhesitatingly sacrifices himself in tackles and never gives up.

MIDFIELD

Maxi Rodríguez, formerly a player with Liverpool, is still a spirited midfielder. Regular midfield comrades are Éver Banega with Valencia and Fernando Gago with Boca Juniors.

THE SOPHISTICATED ONE

Ángel Di María was born 1988 in Rosario, just like Messi. María joined Benfica in Portugal and left for Real Mardid in 2010. Di María is a sophisticated and graceful attacking midfielder and even a winger; he sets up goals and scores goals.

THE COACH

Under coach Alejandro Sabella, Argentina won silver at the 2014 World Cup in Brazil, and Messi was voted Best Player. Sabella then left and his place at the helm was taken by Gerardo Martino, who had previously coached for the Paraguayan national team, Newell's Old Boys in Argentina, and Spanish giants Barcelona.

AGÜERO

Sergio Agüero was born in 1988 in a suburb of Buenos Aires. He began his career with the team Independiente in Argentina but traveled to Spain at the age of 18 to join Atlético Madrid. There his star began to properly shine as a goalscorer and was bought by the billionaire team Manchester City in 2011.

Agüero is an unstoppable attacker; he has vast explosive power and is always dangerous. Messi says that Agüero is endowed with "incredible power and strength" and that he is incredibly diligent.

Agüero is called "Kun" which is a cartoon character in Argentina and was his favorite when he was a child. Agüero was for a time married to Diego Maradona's daughter and together they have a son, Benjamin. If soccer talents are inherited, then it can be expected that Agüero's little son and Maradona's grandson has great potential for the future!

AGÜERO
B. 1988
National games since 2006: 47
Goals: 21*

HIGUAÍN
B. 1987
National games since 2009: 35
Goals: 21*

HIGUAÍN

Gonzalo Higuaín was born in 1987 in France where his father played professional soccer. Higuaín began his career at home in Argentina with River Plate but was transferred to Real Madrid at the age of twenty. Higuaín remained with Real Madrid until the summer of 2013 when he traveled to Napoli in Italy to join their legendary team.

Higuaín played his first national game in 2009 and has been a permanent member of the team since then. Higuaín is a cunning attacker with an eye for goals, and with him, Agüero, and Messi in the front lines, the Argentines will have few problems gathering goals in the future.

*Numbers as of September 2014.

Learn More!

Books

- *Messi: The Inside Story of the Boy who Became a Legend,* by Luca Caioli
  An insightful, well-written, and entertaining biography.
- *The Flea: The Amazing Story of Leo Messi,* by Michael Part
  Everything you'd want to know about the soccer genius.

Websites

- The Wikipedia entry on Messi holds an abundance of information about the player, his life, teammates, and soccer results.
- espnfc.com (Soccernet)
- goal.com
- 101greatgoals.com
- fcbarcelona.com
- messi.com (A fan page)

Glossary

Striker: A forward player positioned closest to the opposing goal who has the primary role of receiving the ball from teammates and delivering it to the goal.

Winger: The player who keeps to the margins of the field and receives the ball from midfielders or defenders and then sends it forward to the awaiting strikers.

Offensive midfielder: This player is positioned behind the team's forwards and seeks to take the ball through the opposing defense. They either pass to the strikers or attempt a goal themselves. This position is sometimes called "number 10" in reference to the Brazilian genius Pelé, who more or less created this role and wore shirt number 10.

Defensive midfielder: Usually plays in front of his team's defense. The player's central role is to break the offense of the opposing team and deliver the ball to their team's forwards. The contribution of these players is not always obvious but they nevertheless play an important part in the game.

Central midfielder: The role of the central midfielder is divided between offense and defense. The player mainly seeks to secure the center of the field for their team. Box-to-box midfielders are versatile players who possess such strength and foresight that they constantly spring between the penalty areas.

Fullbacks (either left back or right back): Players who defend the sides of the field, near their own goal, but also dash up the field overlapping with wingers in order to lob the ball into the opponent's goal. The fullbacks are sometimes titled wing backs if they are expected to play a bigger role in the offense.

Center backs: These players are the primary defenders of their teams, and are two or three in number depending on formation. The purpose of the center backs is first and foremost to prevent the opponents from scoring and then send the ball towards the center.

Sweeper: The original purpose of the sweeper was to stay behind the defending teammates and "sweep up" the ball if they happened to lose it, but also to take the ball forward. The position of the sweeper has now been replaced by defensive midfielders.

Goalkeeper: Prevents the opponent's goals and is the only player who is allowed to use their hands!

Coach: _____

Pick Your Team!

Who do you want on the field with Messi?
Pick your team and don't forget the coach!

Goalkeeper: _____

Right back: _____

Left back: _____

Defender: _____

Defender: _____

Midfielder: _____

Midfielder: _____

Midfielder: _____

Forward:
MESSI _____

Forward: _____

Forward: _____

The Messi Board Game!

Play with one die

Play to win!

And we're off!

2

The coach thinks you're too small and doesn't let you play. Wait 1 round.

You score the first goal with the school team. Go forward 4 places.

5

You're too shy to go to Barcelona. Go back 4 places.

You become the main star in La Masia. Go forward 3 places.

8

You're in the starting 11 but get injured. Wait 1 round.

You score a hat trick for the first time. Go forward 3 places.

11

You provide a beautiful assist to Gudjohnsen who scores. Roll again.

You become champion with Barcelona. Go forward 4 places!

14

Argentina loses in the World Cup. You are devastated. Wait 2 rounds.